ELMHURST PUBLIC LIBRARY

3 1135 01926 3422

W9-COJ-941

Italy

Tradition, Culture, and Daily Life

MAJOR NATIONS IN A GLOBAL WORLD

Books in the Series

J
945
Cen

Italy

Tradition, Culture, and Daily Life

MAJOR NATIONS IN A GLOBAL WORLD

Michael Centore

ELMHURST PUBLIC LIBRARY
125 S. Prospect Avenue
Elmhurst, IL 60126-3298

Mason Crest

Mason Crest
450 Parkway Drive, Suite D
Broomall, PA 19008
www.masoncrest.com

Copyright @ 2016 by Mason Crest, an imprint of National Highlights, Inc. All rights reserved. No part of this publication may be reproduced or transmitted in any form or by any means, electronic or mechanical, including photocopying, recording, taping, or any information storage and retrieval system, without permission from the publisher.

Printed and bound in the United States of America.

First printing
9 8 7 6 5 4 3 2 1

Series ISBN: 978-1-4222-3339-9
ISBN: 978-1-4222-3346-7
ebook ISBN: 978-1-4222-8586-2

The Library of Congress has cataloged the hardcopy format(s) as follows:

Library of Congress Cataloging-in-Publication Data

Centore, Michael, 1980-
  Italy / by Michael Centore.
      pages cm. -- (Major nations in a global world: tradition, culture, and daily life)
  Includes index.

   ISBN 978-1-4222-3346-7 (hardback) -- ISBN 978-1-4222-3339-9 (series) -- ISBN 978-1-4222-8586-2 (ebook)
 1. Italy--Juvenile literature. 2. Italy--Social life and customs--Juvenile literature. I. Title.
 DG451.C438 2015
 945--dc23
                                2015005030

Developed and produced by MTM Publishing, Inc.
        Project Director   Valerie Tomaselli
        Copyeditor   Lee Motteler/Geomap Corp.
        Editorial Coordinator Andrea St. Aubin

Indexing Services   Andrea Baron, Shearwater Indexing

Art direction and design by Sherry Williams, Oxygen Design Group

Contents

KEY ICONS TO LOOK FOR:

 Words to Understand: These words with their easy-to-understand definitions will increase the reader's understanding of the text, while building vocabulary skills.

 Sidebars: This boxed material within the main text allows readers to build knowledge, gain insights, explore possibilities, and broaden their perspectives by weaving together additional information to provide realistic and holistic perspectives.

 Research Projects: Readers are pointed toward areas of further inquiry connected to each chapter. Suggestions are provided for projects that encourage deeper research and analysis.

 Text-Dependent Questions: These questions send the reader back to the text for more careful attention to the evidence presented there.

 Series Glossary of Key Terms: This back-of-the book glossary contains terminology used throughout this series. Words found here increase the reader's ability to read and comprehend higher-level books and articles in this field.

The ancient theatre of Taormina in Sicily, in southern Italy.

INTRODUCTION

Italy is a nation of great geographical and cultural beauty. From the breathtaking peaks of the Alps in the north to the lush vegetation and clear blue waters of the Amalfi Coast in the south, the country is home to many stunning vistas. It has been at the center of some of the most profound changes in human civilization, especially considering its rich history as the seat of the Roman Empire. And the Italian Renaissance remains an example of humankind's highest intellectual and artistic abilities.

Today Italy is home to some 60 million residents. Few countries maintain such a vibrant living connection to their past. The daily life of Italians is informed by traditions that have been in place for centuries, such as an agricultural and gastronomic heritage of food and wine. Even so, Italy continues to forge ahead into the twenty-first century as part of the European Union. Its economy continues to diversify as it contributes to a globalized world economy. In recent years, Italy has pioneered production of alternative and renewable energies, especially wind and solar power. Such an innovative spirit is essential as Italy works to uphold its unique culture while meeting the challenges of the modern world.

The Forum
in Rome.

WORDS TO UNDERSTAND

autonomy: the right of self-government.

codify: to classify things and organize them into systems.

entity: an existing thing.

imperial: relating to an empire or an emperor.

indigenous: something produced, growing, living, or occurring. naturally in a particular region or environment.

parliament: a body of government responsible for enacting laws.

CHAPTER 1

History, Religion, and Tradition

The history of Italy is as complicated as it is fascinating. Various political, **imperial**, and religious forces have shaped the culture of this nation. The process has spanned the history of Western civilization, making Italy a unique bridge between ancient and modern worlds.

Among the first recorded groups who lived in Italy were the Etruscans. The Etruscans settled on the west-central coast of Italy, primarily in the area of present-day Tuscany. The Etruscans had their own language, and inscriptions date the origins of their culture to 800 BCE. Their civilization flourished for several hundred years. They produced artwork such as intricately decorated pots and vases, pioneered mining techniques, and organized a network of city-states that spread far south of Rome by the sixth century BCE.

One type of Etruscan pottery, such as this replica of an amphora (vase), was influenced by ancient Greek ceramic work originating in Athens, known as the "black figure" style.

ECHOES OF THE ETRUSCANS

Since the Etruscans left very few texts—mostly inscriptions on pottery or tombstones—scholars still have great difficulty comprehending their vocabulary.

This period was the height of Etruscan civilization. By the end of the century, Rome had grown in power, and in 509 BC the Romans overthrew the Etruscan leadership. This event marked the beginning of the Roman Republic. A republic is a form of government in which citizens elect representatives to govern for them. Political principles developed during the Roman Republic, such as the separation of powers between branches of government, have had lasting influence on Western societies. Even the U.S. Constitution is partly modeled on the Roman model. The Roman Republic spanned over 450 years, gradually widening its influence over places as far away as North Africa, the Iberian Peninsula, and present-day France. Such growing power abroad paved the way for the transition from a republic to the Roman Empire.

Perhaps no political **entity** has shaped the history and culture of Western civilization so much as the Roman Empire. Most historians agree that the empire began when the Roman Senate appointed Julius Caesar "perpetual dictator" in 44 BC Thirteen years later, Caesar's nephew Augustus became the first official emperor of Rome. During his rule he oversaw a vast building program, constructing or restoring over eighty temples in a single year. The arts, agriculture, and the economy began to flourish, leading to a two-hundred-year period known as the Pax Romana, or "Roman peace." By the second century CE, the empire had peaked in size: it covered well over 2 million square miles, encircling the Mediterranean Sea, and had a population of 60 to 70 million citizens.

The empire grew so unwieldy that Emperor Diocletian divided it in half in 285 CE, This led to the creation of the Eastern Roman Empire and the Western Roman Empire. The differences in traditions between the two halves of the empire would give each a unique identity over time. The Western Roman Empire would remain Latin speaking, while the Eastern Roman (or Byzantine) Empire

This 1870 map of the Roman Empire shows it "in its greatest extent."

would adopt the Greek tongue. In 330 CE, Emperor Constantine relocated the capital of the empire from Rome to the city of Byzantium (at the site of Istanbul in present-day Turkey) in the East. He renamed the city Constantinople, and the move signaled a shift of power that would ultimately weaken the West. With the military no longer united, the West was susceptible to foreign invasion. In 476 CE the Germanic soldier Odoacer conquered the empire and became the first king of Italy. This transition marked the unofficial end of the Western Roman Empire, though the Byzantine Empire continued on for another thousand years.

GOVERNING THE ROMAN REPUBLIC

The government of the Roman Republic was divided into three branches: the consuls, the Senate, and the Assembly. The consuls were two high-powered officials who ran the government in one-year terms. The Senate was made up of aristocrats appointed by the consuls to help direct the affairs of the republic. The Assembly was composed of citizens elected by the consuls. They voted on laws and served as the voice of the people.

Pont du Gard ("bridge over the River Gardon"), which is part of a massive irrigation system in southeastern France, is one of the biggest examples today of ancient Roman engineering.

The legacy of the Roman Empire in Western culture is impossible to overstate. Modern conveniences that we often take for granted, such as indoor plumbing, have their origins in the Roman Empire, as do agricultural advances such as irrigation systems. Romans developed and codified legal concepts such as the right to property that remain the foundation for Western societies. Architects still utilize building details perfected by the Romans, while writers build upon Roman literary techniques. Latin, the language of the Romans, is the basis of many modern European languages. Even modern Italians' love of wine can be traced to their country's Roman ancestors.

After Constantine converted to Christianity in the early fourth century, the empire grew steadily more aligned with the religion. In the year 800, Pope Leo III made the Frankish king Charlemagne Western Roman emperor, thus beginning the era of the Holy Roman Empire. This very complicated assembly of kingdoms, papal states (properties belonging to the Catholic Church), and other smaller territories was designed to recapture the past glory of the Roman Empire and uphold Christian ideals. However, constant disputes between landowners and conflicts of interest between the Church and the emperor made these goals impossible. Though the Holy Roman Empire was not officially dissolved until 1806, it was marked by confusion throughout.

HOLY ROMAN EMPIRE?

Due to the Holy Roman Empire's ever-shifting alliances between and among territories, the French philosopher Voltaire once quipped that it "was neither holy, nor Roman, nor an empire."

In response to this chaotic environment, Italy saw the rise of city-states in the Middle Ages. Urban centers such as Venice, Florence, and Milan were able to increase their wealth through trade. This led to greater independence from both the emperor and the pope, so that city-states could begin to govern themselves. In time, the economic success and **autonomy** of these city-states, and the powerful families that controlled them, created conditions for the Italian Renaissance to flourish. Families such as the Medici in Florence beginning in the late 1400s were able to support artists such as Leonardo da Vinci and

One of the most famous of all Renaissance artworks, Michelangelo's *The Creation of Adam*, part of the Sistine Chapel in Vatican City.

Michelangelo, leading to triumphs in art, engineering, literature, and other fields that would redefine Western thought.

The Renaissance was not to last, as the rising power of neighboring empires threatened the existence of the city-states. First the Spanish Empire ruled, followed by the Austrian and French empires. Fed up with the incompetence of foreign rule, Italian citizens began clamoring for independence. Charismatic leaders such as Giuseppe Mazzini and Giuseppe Garibaldi led the movement known as the Risorgimento ("resurgence") in the mid-nineteenth century. With the cooperation of members of the monarchy, as well as aid from foreign armies, Garibaldi's forces were able to drive out the lingering Austrian and Spanish presence. In 1861, the new Kingdom of Italy was recognized as a unified nation-state. Further territories were added later in the decade. With the capture of Rome from the pope's authority in 1870, the Risorgimento was complete. Rome was made the official capital of Italy one year later, and the modern Italian state was born.

THE HEART OF ITALY

Giuseppe Mazzini was nicknamed "The Beating Heart of Italy" for his tireless efforts to bring the nation together.

With the modernization of Italy came a wave of industrialization, though areas south of Naples remained largely agrarian. In 1915 Italy entered World War I on the side of the Allies, but in 1922 the fascist Benito Mussolini took power, quickly turning Italy into a dictatorship. In 1929 Mussolini established Vatican City in Rome as an independent city-state and headquarters of the Roman Catholic Church; while Catholicism is no longer the sole state-supported religion of Italy, Vatican City's role in international relations continues to make it—and the pope—prevalent forces in Italian life. Italy originally stayed out of World War II, but Mussolini's pact with German dictator Adolf Hitler forced its entrance; unprepared for the intensity of the fighting, the Italians fell to the Allies in 1943, and Mussolini was executed two years later. In 1946 Italy became a republic, governed by a prime minister and **parliament**, and while it has seen both periods of economic growth and political instability, it remains a vital component of the European Union today.

In Rome, the Palazzo Montecitorio is where one house of Italy's parliament, the Chamber of Deputies, meets.

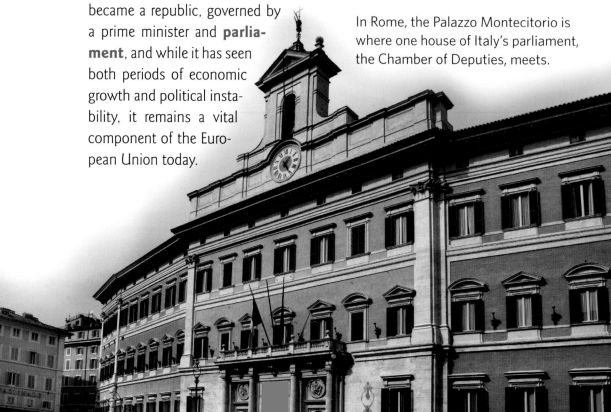

TEXT-DEPENDENT QUESTIONS

1. What are some lasting contributions of the Roman Empire to Western society?
2. Was the Holy Roman Empire a cohesive political organization? Why or why not?
3. What factors led to the rise of city-states in Italy?

RESEARCH PROJECTS

1. Select a Roman emperor and write a short biography of his life, emphasizing his contributions to the empire.
2. Find a painting, poem, or other work from the Italian Renaissance and research the history of its creation. Write an appreciation of the work, including the story of its origin.

Statue of Augustus Caesar.

Sharing a meal, Italian style.

WORDS TO UNDERSTAND

defray: to reduce the cost of.

intergenerational: existing between different generations.

patriarch: the male head of a household.

secular: relating to worldly concerns; not religious.

sustainable: describes a method of farming that tries not to deplete resources or damage the natural environment.

CHAPTER 2

Family and Friends

Italians are a very social people. Many populate the cafés and piazzas, or central squares, of their cities and towns throughout the day, meeting up with friends, checking out the scene, and carrying on long discussions about all sorts of topics. In fact, conversation is seen as something of an art form, and nowhere is it more readily practiced than amongst one's family and friends.

The family is the most important unit of Italian social life. Traditionally, Italian families are large, with five or more children. This was especially true when the country was primarily agricultural, and families depended on their children's help for farming, cooking, and other household tasks. The tie between family and land

Piazzas and other public spaces are common meeting grounds for friends and family, as this scene in the square surrounding the cathedral in Milan shows.

dates back as far as the fifth century BCE, when farms in Rome were often small, sustainable operations owned and operated by single families.

SPEAKING WITH YOUR HANDS!

Conversations among friends and family in Italy are always punctuated with hand gestures. Rubbing your thumb and forefinger together indicates money, tucking a flat hand beneath your chin shows that you are fed up with something, and rapidly pinching and releasing the fingers near the chest means that something is fearful. One professor has categorized 250 different Italian conversational gestures!

Over the past century, the Italian economy has become more industrial. While there is still a great deal of agriculture, it is typically done on a larger scale than in the past. Increased mobility means that children can now leave their hometowns to pursue work elsewhere. Women now take on employment, whereas previously they were devoted to childrearing and domestic chores. All of this has led to changes in the structure of the Italian family. With both parents working, couples are now having fewer children. There is a greater balance between maternal and paternal authority, rather than the traditional notion of the Italian "patriarch" who made all the decisions for a given home.

Despite these shifts, the importance of the family remains deeply embedded in Italian culture. Most families will gather at least once a day for a communal meal. Even if children leave home, they maintain close contact with their families, sometimes calling them daily to exchange news. Rather than send elder parents to assisted living centers, Italian sons and daughters often still opt to care for them directly. Family members know they can turn to one another in times of trouble, an unspoken pact that binds them together in a way other social institutions cannot. Such closeness is true among immigrant Italian families as well. For example, many Italian American families still uphold the sense of intergenerational closeness inherited from their ancestors.

FAMILIES MEETING FAMILIES

When one Italian family invites another over for dinner, it is seen as a formal occasion. The guest is expected to bring a small gift such as flowers or chocolates to offer the host family, and a follow-up thank you note the next day is essential.

Nothing quite brings an Italian family together like a major family event. Births, baptisms, and weddings are especially festive occasions. While traditional Italians do not have baby showers to prepare for the new arrival, friends

Women are more involved in the workforce than ever before. In Milan, two women—using a motorcycle and a bicycle—move about their busy lives.

Despite the increasing demands of modern life, Italian families still get together frequently for meals. This couple prepares for a typical family gathering.

and relatives are expected to provide strong emotional support. For example, it was once a common practice to select a woman close to the family to act as a midwife during the birth. It is customary to name the firstborn son and daughter after the paternal grandfather and grandmother, respectively. This creates a living link to the family's history.

According to tradition, within a few months of the birth, the child is baptized at the local Catholic church. This is a celebratory affair, not quite on the scale of a wedding but with the same festive spirit. The parents select godparents for the child whom they can trust to impart moral and spiritual guidance. A special baptismal gown is purchased for the ceremony—blue for boys, pink for girls—and the infant is blessed with holy water while friends and family look on. Afterwards, a large party is held at the parents' home. Guests lavish the child with gifts and partake of plenty of home-cooked food. It is actually considered bad luck to serve store-bought food on this special day.

The Italian funeral traditions also take place in Catholic churches, where masses for the dead are celebrated. One unique Italian funeral tradition is the making of posters to commemorate the deceased. The posters, known as *annunci mortuari*, are hung around town to alert residents of the person's passing.

Italian weddings are vibrant affairs and include the extended families of both bride and groom. In more traditional families, the groom must ask the bride's father privately for permission to marry the man's daughter. This is considered a sign of respect for the integrity of the family unit. If the man consents, then wedding plans are underway.

On the night before the wedding, an intimate dinner is held with those closest to the bride and groom, much like in the United States. Traditionally, the bride wears something green to this event as a symbol of health and fertility. She spends the night at her parents' house and accompanies the groom to the church the following morning, where an early Mass precedes the wedding service. It is customary to break a glass after the ceremony; the number of shards represents the number of years the couple will be happily married. It is also common practice to shower the bride and groom with confetti as they exit the church and to release doves. If the bride and groom are to travel to the reception via car, members of the wedding party will have adorned the front grill with flowers.

A typical reception includes lots of food—antipasto (a sampling of Italian appetizers such as olives, prosciutto, and cheese), a classic "wedding soup" made of green vegetables and meat, and hearty main courses such as veal and pasta. A dessert called *wanda*, bowtie-shaped twists of fried dough dusted with sugar, symbolizes the sweetness of the new couple's married life. Wine and coffee are staple beverages. Instead of cake, which is rarely served in Italy, sugar-coated almonds complete the meal. To help finance this lavish party, guests will place money in a satin bag the bride carries with her known as *la borsa*. To show their gratitude, the bride and groom will pass out a small gift called a *confetti bomboniera* at the end of the reception.

Specialties served at Italian weddings: from left, traditional Italian wedding soup, almond candies for the *confetti bomboniera.* and fried dough called *wanda*.

GATHERING AT THE TABLE

An Italian proverb beautifully sums up the importance of friends and family in Italian culture: *"A tavola non si invecchia."* In English, this means, "At the table one does not grow old."

Getting to the church for a wedding ceremony is not at all a private affair in this square in Amalfi, on the west-central coast of Italy.

Italy is a country of strong regional identities, and these include wedding traditions. In Calabria, the groom's friends will play a practical joke on him by taking his tie, tearing it into small pieces, and "selling" the pieces to guests to help defray honeymoon expenses. Another Calabrian tradition involves ordering trays of pastries, coffee, and champagne to the homes of the bride and groom on the morning of the wedding. In Venice, the bride traditionally would not wear her wedding dress when traveling to the ceremony, putting it on only when arriving at the church—or, in some cases, not until her first dance at the reception. Though some of these traditions have fallen out of favor, they are nonetheless reminders of the importance of weddings in Italian culture.

TEXT-DEPENDENT QUESTIONS

1. What factors have led to Italian families becoming smaller over time?

2. How do modern Italian families maintain their sense of closeness?

3. What are some regional Italian wedding traditions?

RESEARCH PROJECTS

1. Research some of the differences between the northern and southern parts of Italy. How did they become different? Have these differences led to alternate approaches to family and social life?

2. Select a social event such as a birthday, wedding anniversary, baptism, or funeral, and research how Italians traditionally organize the function. Are there special customs that are not found in other countries?

Typical family seaside vacation.

Pasta with meat sauce, a classic Italian dish.

WORDS TO UNDERSTAND

cultivar: a variety of plant that has been intentionally maintained for a period of time.

papal: of or relating to the pope.

sacramental: of or relating to a religious observance, especially of the Christian faith.

tenet: a belief or principle held in common by members of a group.

vintner: a person who makes wine.

CHAPTER 3

Food and Drink

Italians love to eat. So much of their culture is based around the communal meal: food and drink shared with friends and family. Italian **vintners** produce some of the most renowned wines in the entire world. The rich soil and sun of the Mediterranean make for a long, fertile growing season. Each region of the country prides itself on its local products, such as Parmesan, the famous cheese from the city of Parma, or the hearty red wine from the Chianti area of Tuscany.

One beverage the Italians are crazy about is coffee. Coffee is not native to Italy. Middle Eastern merchants who traded in Venice introduced it to the city in the sixteenth century. At first, advisors close to Pope Clement VIII urged him

Food brings Italians together, whether in restaurants, at the homes of friends and family, or simply at their own dinner table to enjoy good food.

to ban the drink, as it was closely related to the Islamic Ottoman Empire. But after tasting his first espresso in 1600, Clement was so taken by the flavor that he gave it his **papal** approval. Coffeehouses began opening to serve Venetians hooked on the beverage. The trend spread to nearby cities such as Milan and Turin, and the place of coffee in Italian culture continued to grow.

Today, coffee is a cornerstone of an Italian's daily routine. There are all sorts of coffee drinks, some specific to certain times of day. What most Americans think of as an "espresso" is actually the standard cup of coffee in Italy, called a caffè. This is a very small, strong cup of coffee that can be swilled in a single shot. Cappuccino is an espresso served with frothy steamed milk on top. Macchiato is a smaller version of cappuccino: an espresso with just a drop of steamed milk. For the brave, the *caffè stretto* is a highly concentrated espresso made with less water than the standard *caffè*.

Caffè, or what is also known as espresso, is a small cup of intensely flavored coffee and a standard beverage in Italy.

One of the best-known regional specialties of Italy, Parmesan cheese can be grated fine to be sprinkled on a pasta sauce. It can also be eaten on its own in small chunks, sometimes accompanied with bread and olives.

Wine also varies by region, some of which specialize in white or red. Chianti, a hardy red wine, is one of the most celebrated wines of Italy.

ITALIAN FOR "COFFEE"

The Italian word for coffee, *caffè*, is the same word used for a café where coffee is served. In the *caffè*, many patrons choose to drink their coffee standing up at a long bar rather than sit at a table.

Whether Italians are enjoying a morning cappuccino or an evening meal, one thing remains the same: they do not like to be rushed. When the fast-food chain McDonald's was preparing to open a restaurant near the Spanish Steps in Rome in 1986, a group of Italians protested. They felt the culture of fast food went against the Italian reverence for food and drink. Out of these protests, the Slow Food movement was born.

The central **tenets** of the Slow Food movement are the preservation of traditional and regional foods; the cultivation of fruits, vegetables, livestock, and other food sources native to local ecosystems; and the right of all people to savor these native cuisines. Throughout the years, Slow Food has hosted many events promoting sustainable foods and good nutrition. In 2004 the movement even opened its own academic institution, the University of Gastronomic Sciences in Pollenzo, in the northwestern part of Italy, to provide instruction in the relationship between agriculture and gastronomy. While the Slow Food movement is headquartered in the neighboring town of Bra, it has expanded to over a 100,000 members across 150 countries worldwide.

One of the Italian specialties no doubt important to the Slow Food movement is pasta. This noodle-type product made from durum wheat and water (or

eggs) is a staple in the Italian diet, so much so that Italians eat over sixty pounds of it per person per year! Legend has it that Italian explorer Marco Polo discovered pasta during his travels in China and brought it back to his native land in the thirteenth century. While he may have helped popularize the dish, noodles in Italy actually date back to Roman and Etruscan times. Pasta's longtime popularity is attributed to the fact that it stores easily, is inexpensive to produce and purchase, and can be used in a variety of ways. Each region in Italy has its own distinctive pasta shapes and sauces. It is worth noting that tomato sauce is a relatively recent discovery, dating from the mid-nineteenth century.

Pasta comes in many different shapes and preparations and is usually enjoyed as the *primi,* or first dish, in a meal. This man is preparing ravioli, a pasta stuffed with cheese.

Though various regions throughout Italy are known for their own pasta dishes, as well as cheeses and cured meats, it is two liquid products—olive oil and wine—that form the basis of Italian culinary identity. Olive oil is a staple in the Mediterranean diet, produced in great quantities in Spain, Italy, and Greece, as well as North Africa and the countries of the eastern Mediterranean. In the eighth century BCE, a wave of Greek emigration brought olive trees to southern Italy, and with this came the beginnings of Italian olive oil production.

"LIQUID GOLD"

Olive oil was "liquid gold" to the Greek poet Homer. The Greek physician Hippocrates, the "father of medicine," referred to it as "the great therapeutic." To many Italians and residents of the Mediterranean, it is simply "the nectar of the gods."

Producing olive oil in the traditional method is a very labor intensive process. Olives are easily damaged and must be handpicked or shaken free with rakes or other nonmechanical tools to ensure freshness. No later than a day after being picked, the farmer brings his olives to the communal mill, called a *frantoio*. Via a series of mechanical processes, the olives are washed, ground, mixed, and pressed. After excess water is removed, the resulting oil is stored in steel tanks until it is ready for bottling. Due to the uniqueness of different **cultivars** of olives, each region has its own particular oil. Some are lighter and fruitier in taste, while others are heavier and fuller bodied.

OLIVE OIL AND HEALTH

Olive oil consumption in the United States has grown tremendously over the past few decades as people have become more aware of its health properties. According to many researchers, olive oil can help prevent heart disease, lower cholesterol, and improve the immune system, among other benefits.

Today, Italy is the second largest producer of olive in the world, behind Spain. Similar to olive oil, wine was among the first internationally traded products in Western civilization, and the wines of Italy have played a key role throughout. When the same Greek emigrants who introduced the olive tree to Southern Italy saw the fertility of their adopted home, they began to import

This olive grower harvests the raw olives by hand; fresh off the tree, olives are very bitter and must be cured—usually in brine (a salt mixture)—to make them edible.

Workers in the Piedmont region, in Italy's northwest, picking during the grape harvest, a ritual during the fall for winemakers throughout Italy.

vines and make wine around the eighth century BCE With the growth of the Roman Empire, the demand for wine only rose, and production was flourishing by the second century BCE.

Italy is currently the world's largest producer by volume, with over a million vineyards in cultivation. There are twenty wine regions in the country, each known for a specific type of wine. In the north, Friuli-Venezia and Veneto are known for their white wines, particularly those made from the pinot grigio grape; further south, Tuscany's Chianti region produces a series of bold red wines; and in the far south and Sicily, the island off the southwest tip of Italy, native varieties of grape such as the Nero d'Avola have surged in popularity in recent years. Along with plenty of fresh-baked bread, a bottle of wine has remained a fixture on the Italian family table for centuries.

MIX IT UP

While today's Italian wine drinkers often refrain from mixing flavoring agents into their wine, Romans were not averse to adding honey, spices, salt water, and even chalk (to cut acidity).

TEXT-DEPENDENT QUESTIONS

1. What are some examples of Italian coffee beverages?
2. What do members of the Slow Food movement hope to accomplish? Do you think their ideas would benefit our modern world? Why or why not?
3. How does the cultivation of wine and olive oil help Italians stay connected to their national identity?

RESEARCH PROJECTS

1. Research a specific vineyard in a wine-growing region of Italy. Find out what type of wine they produce, how they produce it, and what makes it special.
2. Seek out any local food supplier in your area (such as a farmer, winemaker, or cheese maker) and research their history and means of production.

Standard ingredients used in Italian cuisine.

View of historic Bologna, Italy.

WORDS TO UNDERSTAND

artisanal: describing something produced on a small scale, usually handmade.

fabricate: to construct or manufacture something.

luminary: a person of prominence or great achievement.

lustrous: having a bright, radiant sheen.

testament: a tangible proof of something.

CHAPTER 4

School, Work, and Industry

Italians are a naturally industrious people. Known for their advances in art, engineering, and design, they place a high value on well-made items. They understand the importance of education so that one may learn the history, tradition, and practical techniques of one's chosen field. To the Italians, the act of making or doing something well is its own reward, and every profession has a certain nobility.

Elementary and high school systems in Italy are similar to those of other European countries. Education is free for all students, including public nursery schools. Students are required to attend school from age six through sixteen. The first formal level is primary school, which students attend between the ages of six and ten. Following this is first lower secondary school, attended between ages of eleven and fourteen; then upper secondary school, attended from fourteen onward. Upper secondary school is equivalent to American high school. After the first two years, students have the option of enrolling in more specialized schools focusing on particular subjects such as the fine arts, sciences, or classics. They may also choose to enroll in a technical or preprofessional school to learn a specific vocation.

Today approximately 85,000 students attend all the campuses of the University of Bologna. In this photo, students, residents, and tourists mingle in the streets leading from the main square—Piazza Maggiore—near the main campus, making Bologna one of the most vibrant university cities in the world.

Upon completion of upper secondary school, some students elect to go on to the university level. A popular destination is the University of Bologna, the oldest continually operating university in the Western world. In 1088, independent scholars began teaching in Bologna. Students came to Bologna to study with these scholars, paying them in donations rather than a set tuition. Over the next few centuries, the university became a center for the study of law, drawing scholars from the farthest reaches of Europe. These scholars organized themselves into loose collectives based on their country of origin. Gradually these collectives came to associate as a single unit that would become what we know as the University of Bologna. As of 2013, the university offered 200 degree programs and had five satellite campuses, including one in Buenos Aires, Argentina.

BOLOGNA'S STAR STUDENTS

Some famous scholars who have spent time at the University of Bologna include Thomas Becket, the Archbishop of Canterbury from 1162 to 1170; architect, poet, and philosopher Leon Battista Alberti; and famed astronomer Nicolaus Copernicus.

Just as revered as scholastic accomplishments in Italy are the fields of art and design. Small-scale industries such as papermaking and ceramics are excellent examples of how these trades continue to flourish, making Italy a worldwide leader in the preservation of traditional art forms.

A sample of the fine art paper made by contemporary manufacturers in Venice.

Paper was discovered in China early in the first century AD The technique of papermaking spread to the Arab world. From there it came to Amalfi, a coastal town in southern Italy, via trading routes in the eleventh century. It is a highly labor intensive process, involving pulping, pressing, and hand drying a mixture of fiber and water. In the Amalfi region, only the purest mountain water was used, resulting in papers noted for their durability. While the Industrial Revolution forced many of the paper mills to close in the nineteenth century, a small but devoted band of artisans managed to preserve the trade. Today, few of the original mills remain, and one has been turned into a museum that

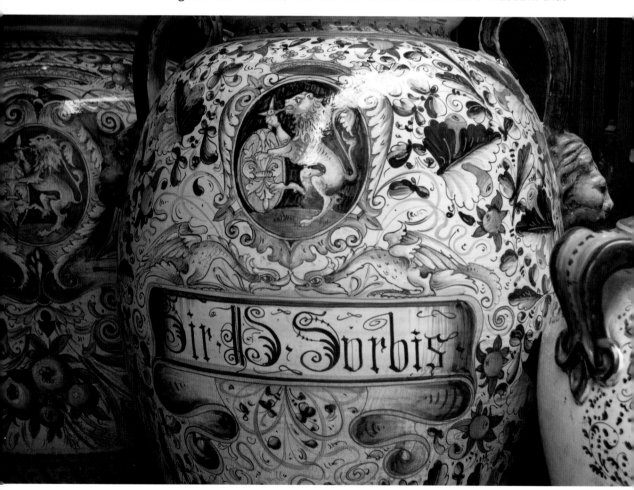

Contemporary versions of majolica, an Italian style of ceramics dating back to the fourteenth century.

demonstrates these old, **artisanal** techniques. However, a new generation of papermakers, printers, and bookbinders has sprung up in cities farther north, such as Florence and Venice.

A LABORIOUS PROCESS

Using traditional techniques from the Middle Ages, it can take up to twenty-four hours to make a single sheet of paper! Italians also excel at paper marbling, which is the technique of producing colorful patterns on paper using ink, paint, and chemical solutions. These individual sheets can be used as endpapers in books or to wrap gifts.

Italian ceramics have a similarly rich history. The ancient Greeks introduced their techniques of sculpting and firing functional pottery such as jugs and vases to southern Italy in the fourth and fifth centuries BCE. By 1350, traders were bringing a new type of **lustrous**, decorated ceramic into Italy known as majolica. Italians began to create their own majolica, embellishing the designs with historical and mythological imagery.

Though the majolica industry reached its apex during the Renaissance, ceramicists in the town of Deruta in the region of Umbria continue to produce some of the finest pieces in the world. Deruta has been a center for ceramics since the Middle Ages. Today there are over 200 ceramics workshops, as well as a ceramics museum and school. The creation of a single piece of majolica is a complicated endeavor involving sculpting, glazing, painting, and multiple firings. All of this is done by hand.

A more current example of Italy's contribution to global industry is Milan's place as an international fashion center. The second largest city in Italy, Milan is located in the Lombardy region. As far back as the Middle Ages, Milan was known for its hand-crafted luxury goods. With the wave of industrialization in the mid-nineteenth century came new modes of production and distribution such as textile factories and department stores. More and more people had access to fashionable items, and people of all economic backgrounds became more fashion conscious. The industry was balanced between larger factories and smaller workshops where tailors made clothing to the customer's exact specifications.

FASHION WEEK IN MILANO

Along with London, New York, and Paris, Milan hosts all-important "fashion weeks" twice a year. These exclusive events give designers a chance to show their latest creations to the world.

It was not for a few decades, however, that Milan truly came into its own as an international fashion capital. To help recover from World War II, the Italian government encouraged the production of leather goods for sale in foreign markets. Certain items such as Italian shoes began to acquire a worldwide reputation. Products **fabricated** in Italy were less expensive than their French counterparts, making them an attractive option for global customers. Even as Florence and Rome were more famous fashion destinations through the 1950s and 1960s, Milan was emerging as a leader in affordable, "ready-to-wear" clothing, drawing both tourists and native Italians to shop there. Since the 1970s, Milan has emerged as the undisputed leader in Italian fashion, with many top designers headquartered in the city. The fashion industry in Italy employs over a million workers.

An exhibition hall with racks of the latest styles from Milan, one of the world's fashion centers.

TEXT-DEPENDENT QUESTIONS

1. In what ways does the success of the University of Bologna demonstrate Italy's commitment to education?

2. How does the production of small-scale items such as handmade paper or ceramics help Italians maintain a connection to their cultural history?

3. What steps did Italy take to become an international leader in the fashion industry?

RESEARCH PROJECTS

1. Research secondary school education in Italy. How is their system different than the one you find in America? How is it similar? After comparing and contrasting the two, list what you think are the pros and cons of each.

2. Research a papermaking factory, ceramics workshop, or fashion house located in Italy. How do they run their business? Do they use a mixture of traditional artisan and modern techniques?

An expert glassblower at work.

A 1955 Lancia Aurelia at the historic car race, Mille Miglia.

WORDS TO UNDERSTAND

connoisseur: one who understands the details, technique, and principles of a particular art form.

discipline: a field of study.

quintessential: the best or most representative example of something.

revere: to show great honor to someone or something.

virtuoso: demonstrating great skill at some endeavor.

CHAPTER 5

Arts and Entertainment

Whether they are sharing a meal with friends and family, appreciating one of their country's artistic masterpieces, or enjoying an evening stroll through their town piazza, Italians take great pleasure in the art of living. This involves a balance between work and leisure time. While Italians value productivity and industriousness, they tend to feel that work should not be the sole focus of one's life. They understand the value of healthy diversions from their day-to-day routines.

One of the most popular of these diversions is the sport of auto racing. The tradition of auto racing in Italy dates back to the beginning of the twentieth century, with the establishment of the Coppa Florio road race in Brescia, Lombardy, in 1900,

Vincenzo Trucco, the winner of the Targa Florio, one of the earliest road races in Italy.

A classic Ferrari Dino GT running in the 2013 rally in Brisighella, Italy, in honor of the great Italian Formula One driver of the 1960s, Lorenzo Bandini.

which paved the way for other car racing, such as the Targa Florio on the island of Sicily in the south in 1906 and the Mille Miglia ("the Thousand Miles") in 1927. The Mille Miglia is a very long, difficult course that drivers must navigate from Bresica to Rome and back again. By mid-century, the sport had grown in international popularity, and Italian automakers led the pack with their innovative designs. Alfa Romeo, Bugatti, and Maserati all produced fast, luxurious vehicles. But perhaps the **quintessential** Italian racecar remains the Ferrari.

Enzo Ferrari was working at Alfa Romero when he decided to start his own racing team in 1929. While the first car he produced in 1937 kept the Alfa Romeo name, it was produced entirely in Ferrari's workshop. Two years later he broke away from Alfa entirely to inaugurate the Ferrari brand. In 1947 he issued the company's definitive model, the 125 S. Its powerful twelve-cylinder engine would become a Ferrari signature. The Ferrari race team enjoyed many successes throughout the next few decades. Between 1994 and 2004, German driver Michael Schumacher won seven Formula One championships behind the wheel of a Ferrari. Italian race fans take great pride in being the home of the company.

THE GRAND PRIX, ITALIAN STYLE

One of the most storied auto races in Italy is the Grand Prix, held each September in the city of Monza. The 3.6-mile (5.8-km) course is legendary for its tight turns that test a driver's agility and confidence behind the wheel.

Auto racing embodies sleekness, grace, and finesse—three qualities abundant in Italian culture, from its fashion to its cutting-edge product design. A much older, but no less **revered** form of entertainment is the Italian village festival. These are gatherings of local communities, no matter how big or small, that often take place in the summer. Village festivals can be in honor of a village's patron saint, commemorate an event of historic importance, or celebrate a certain food. Carnival festivals (or *carnevale* in Italian) date back to the Middle Ages. Some variation of *carnevale* occurs in almost every country with a strong Catholic presence. The most famous Italian *carnevale* takes place in Venice. It features elaborate floats and parades, and participants and spectators alike don colorful masks. It is held forty days prior to Easter, just before the period of fasting known as Lent.

Carnevale in Venice is a colorful affair—with many in the city competing for the most elaborate and fanciful costumes and masks.

Italian village festivals always feature one thing in abundance: food. One festival in the northern village of Sessame is devoted to risotto, an Italian rice dish. Another in Massa Lubrense centers on lemons and lemon-based food and drink such as gelato or *limoncello*, an after-dinner liqueur. For those with adventurous palates, there is even a snail festival in Gesico! At these gatherings, the whole community pitches in to help cook and clean, and any profits made are reinvested into next year's festival. After an afternoon spent eating and drinking, the evening concludes with live music and dancing. Sometimes a fireworks display will cap off the night. No matter what they're celebrating, Italian village festivals remain a way for communities to stay connected, both to their native cultures and to each other.

CELEBRATING SAINT STEPHEN

On December 26, many Italian towns will have a gathering to commemorate Saint Stephen, the first Christian martyr. It is a national holiday, so businesses and offices are closed. Traditions include visiting churches and hospitals in groups, reenacting nativity scenes in the town piazzas, and extending the Christmas celebration with a communal meal.

Any discussion of the arts in Italy is incomplete without reference to the masterpieces of Renaissance sculpture and painting. Works such as Leonardo da Vinci's religious painting *The Last Supper* and Michelangelo's seventeen-foot statue *David* were landmark achievements not just in the realm of the visual arts, but for humanity in general. The *David* was carved between 1501 and 1504. It represents in grand scale the biblical hero who defeated the giant Goliath. Hewn from a single block of marble, the sculpture is noted for its impeccable harmony of proportion. It was intended to be mounted high on the exterior of the cathedral in Florence, but those who saw it agreed it was too beautiful to place there. Instead it was situated outside of the main government building in the city for all to admire.

Like people in many other countries, Italians enjoy unwinding with a film or a television program. Long before such modern media, however, the art form of opera combined dramatic plotlines, stunning costumes, and **virtuoso** musical performances to give spectators a similarly entertaining experience. Opera,

The Italian festival of Massa Lubrense celebrates the pleasures of lemons, including the drink known as *limoncello*, pictured here.

which means "work" in Italian, remains a national passion today. Italian operas are among the most performed in the world.

The origins of opera date back to the sixteenth century. In Florence, a group of musicians, poets, and other artists and intellectuals were interested in combining various artistic **disciplines** to create a new form of expression. The result of their collaborations was *Dafne*, a musical work based upon the Greek myth of Apollo and Daphne. Instead of the dialogue being spoken, it was sung. The composer Claudio Monteverdi built upon this template when he wrote *La Favola d'Orfeo* (*The Fable of Orpheus*) in 1607.

OPERA FOR ALL

The Three Tenors—a name given to Luciano Pavarotti, José Carrera, and Plácido Domingo—did much to popularize opera in the late twentieth century. While only one, Pavarotti, was Italian, the group's repertoire included many excerpts from Italian operas.

At first, opera was produced for royal courts and aristocratic audiences. With the opening of the first public opera house in Venice in 1637, that dynamic began to shift. Opera became popular among people of all backgrounds. Traveling opera companies formed to perform new works throughout Italy and other countries in Europe. Composers applied themselves to creating operas to meet the public's demand. Regardless of a composer's place of origin, Italian remained the language of the art form. Themes for operas expanded to include subjects beyond Greek mythology, such as *opera buffa* (comic opera), which utilized everyday language and stripped-down stage sets to tell simple stories that audiences could relate to.

The most famous opera house in the world is La Scala, in Milan. Built in 1778, the venue is known for its incredible acoustics. It has long been the center for Italian opera, and has seen the premieres of works by Verdi, Giuseppi Puccini, and many others.

By the nineteenth century, composers such as Giuseppe Verdi were pushing the limits of opera to new heights. Verdi's style would come to be known as "grand opera": productions with massive casts and usually four or five separate acts. His works managed to appeal to both high-art **connoisseurs** and a general audience. That type of popular reception continues to define Italian opera well into the twenty-first century.

TEXT-DEPENDENT QUESTIONS

1. Why do Italians take such pride in being the home of Ferrari?

2. How do village festivals help bring Italian communities together?

3. What qualities of opera do you think contribute to its continued popularity?

RESEARCH PROJECTS

1. Research another sport that Italians are known to enjoy, such as bicycle racing, tennis, or skiing. Write a summary of its history, including famous participants and major events.

2. Select an Italian opera. Research its development, including any source material the composer used. Write a synopsis of the plot. Specify how the composer may have changed or adapted the material.

Partygoers attend *Carnevale* in Venice.

Ponte Vecchio over the Arno River in Florence.

WORDS TO UNDERSTAND

ecclesiastical: of or relating to a church.

entity: something with an independent, self-contained existence.

figuratively: expressing something metaphorically rather than in a literal sense.

piles: long, slender columns driven into the ground to support a vertical load.

serenity: the quality of utter calmness and quietude.

CHAPTER 6

Cities, Towns, and the Countryside

Being a naturally social people, Italians place great emphasis on public space. As much as it is known for breathtaking natural beauty such as that of the Tuscan hills or the Amalfi Coast, Italy is known for the beauty of its cities, towns, and villages and the landscapes surrounding them. These are the places where Italians live and work, and no two are quite the same. Each one has been shaped by the customs and traditions of its inhabitants over time.

While Venice has a very rich cultural history, it is the city's geographical setting for which it is most famous. Built on 118 small islands scattered across the Venetian Lagoon in the upper Adriatic Sea, the city has an elemental connection to water. Its buildings seem to rise right out of the lagoon. Many are

Left: The Grand Canal in Venice, the city's main "thoroughfare" and a world-renowned signature of Venice's unique urban "landscape."

Right: The job of the gondolier requires rigorous training, and the positions are often passed down from father to son.

built on wooden **piles** that reach down through the water to a base of hard clay. Cutting through the city is a series of canals that function like roadways. The largest of these is the Grand Canal, which snakes through the entire city. Over 400 bridges transverse these canals to facilitate foot traffic, as a large part of Venice is inaccessible by car.

THE WATER IS RISING

Acqua alta ("high water") is a natural phenomenon that occurs in Venice when tides of the Adriatic Sea rise to flood parts of the city. Except in rare instances, the water level is not dangerously high, and Venetians are accustomed to simply waiting for the tide to ebb before continuing their day.

The traditional form of transport in Venice is the gondola. These flat-bottomed rowboats are steered along the canals by men called gondoliers. Today they are mostly used by visitors who wish to experience something of old Venice, though natives will take them to cross waterways if there is no nearby bridge. The proximity to the sea has led to other customs unique to the city. For instance, fish farming is an old Venetian practice. Venetian fishermen study the swimming patterns of fish that enter the lagoon, using centuries-old knowledge of local marine life. They design a series of locks that entrap fish in specific areas so they are easily caught. Anchovies, sea bass, and cuttlefish are just a few of the many types of fish that populate the lagoon.

Italy is unique in having two of the smallest independent nations in the world within its borders: the Vatican and the Republic of San Marino. These entities, also called microstates, are entirely self-governing. While they take up very little land area and have very small populations, they are nonetheless important players in the world of international relations. The Vatican is the world's smallest state, taking up only two-tenths of a square mile. Its population is a scant 770. By comparison, San Marino is much larger, at twenty-four square miles and 29,000 inhabitants.

Despite their independence, their locations ensure that both have active ties to Italy. The Vatican (sometimes referred to as Vatican City) is located in

St. Peter's Square, the heart of the Vatican, an independent Catholic microstate located in Rome, Italy's capital. This view is taken from the dome of the Basilica of St. Peter, likely the most important church in the Roman Catholic world.

Rome. It is built around the famous Basilica of Saint Peter and is the worldwide headquarters of the Catholic Church. When Italy was unified in 1870, the Church lost its Italian territories, known as the Papal States. For years the Holy See, which is the official name for the office of the pope, had no landholdings. Vatican City was established in 1929 as a sovereign state for the Holy See. It is home to such cultural landmarks as the Sistine Chapel, with ceilings painted by Michelangelo. It carries on all manner of diplomatic relations with other countries, with the pope as absolute leader and monarch. Today this is the only such government in all of Europe.

EUROPE'S TINY COUNTRIES

San Marino and Vatican City are not the only microstates in Europe. Andorra, Liechtenstein, Malta, and Monaco are similarly classified.

San Marino is known as the oldest republic in the world. Its origins date to AD 301. Situated high above the surrounding area on the top of Mount Titano in northern Italy, San Marino is literally and figuratively a place apart. Its difficult-to-access location has helped ensure its independence throughout the years. A constitution dating to the late sixteenth century remains the basis for its democratic government. In 1862 it signed a treaty of friendship and cooperation with Italy, setting forth a solid foundation of political and economic partnership.

THE STATUS OF THE MICROSTATES

Both the Vatican and San Marino have their own flags, stamps, and coins. Neither one belongs to the European Union (EU). However, both countries use the euro as the official currency. There has been recent support in San Marino to join the EU, though nothing has been formalized as yet. Because monarchies are prohibited from joining the EU, the Vatican is ineligible.

There are many "hill towns" in Italy similar in appearance to San Marino, such as San Gimignano in the province of Siena in Tuscany. These classic hilltop villages were built above the surrounding countryside for protection against attackers. Other lines of defense included stone walls, gated entrances, and watchtowers to scan the horizon. Because of their geographical limitations,

Located in Tuscany, San Gimignano is one of the most famous hilltop villages in Italy and one of the country's best preserved from the Middle Ages. It is sometimes called the "Manhattan of Tuscany" due to its towers, which recall New York City's skyscrapers.

hill towns are often compact, with narrow streets and stone buildings close together. Many buildings have retained their recognizable reddish-brown tiled roofs, lending them a visual unity. Seaside cliff areas are often built up vertically as well. Towns along the Amalfi Coast, for instance, running from Salerno to Naples on the western side of Italy's boot, are perhaps the best-known example of this adaptive approach to geography.

Regardless of where you are in Italy, you are never far from the centerpiece of **ecclesiastical** architecture, the duomo. "Duomo" is the Italian word for a cathedral; most every city and town of significant size has one, functioning as sacred spaces in which to celebrate the Catholic Mass as well as places of serenity and reflection for residents. They remind one that the landscape of Italy has been shaped by its long association with the Catholic Church. In

These homes are typical of the way people along the Amalfi Coast have adapted to their cliff-side habitat, with narrow streets and houses clinging to rocky walls that rise vertically from the water.

addition to being works of art in and of themselves, duomos often contain artistic treasures, such as the famous Madonnina statue poised atop the cathedral in Milan or Fra Filippo Lippi's frescoes in Spoleto.

A GOTHIC MASTERPIECE

The duomo in Milan is the second largest cathedral in the world, behind that of Seville, Spain. It is a masterpiece of Gothic architecture. Begun in 1386, the official completion date was not for nearly six centuries later: the last gate was installed on January 6, 1965.

The most iconic of the duomos is undoubtedly located in Florence. Officially named the Basilica of Santa Maria del Fiore ("Saint Mary of the Flower"), its bright red octagonal dome and its "striped" façade made of different colored marble are international landmarks. Construction for the cathedral began in 1296, though it took until 1436 to finally complete the dome. The challenge was designing something that had no external supports. Also, as the recipe for concrete had been lost centuries earlier, there was difficulty in selecting the proper building material. Architect Filippo Brunelleschi solved the problem by constructing an inner dome of sandstone and marble that supports the outer dome of red brick. His ingenious solution made him the most celebrated architect of the Renaissance and ensured the prestige of the duomo for centuries to come.

The famous duomo, or cathedral, in Florence, is shown here.

TEXT-DEPENDENT QUESTIONS

1. What are some ways that Venice is different from other cities in Italy?
2. What might be some advantages of being a microstate? What might be some disadvantages?
3. How do duomos contribute to the daily life of Italian cities and towns?

RESEARCH PROJECTS

1. Research another of the European microstates. Write a brief report on your findings, including how it arrived at its independence, how it continues to contribute to world affairs, and some facts about its culture.
2. Research another of Filippo Brunelleschi's architectural projects. Write a brief summary of its history and impact on its surrounding environment.

Aerial view of San Marino.

FURTHER RESEARCH

Online

View statistics, maps, and a brief history about Italy on the Central Intelligence Agency's World Factbook: https://www.cia.gov/library/publications/the-world-factbook/geos/it.html.

Learn more about tourism in Italy by visiting http://www.italia.it/en/home.html.

Find out more about Italy's culture and lifestyle by visiting http://www.lifeinitaly.com/culture.

Check out Lonely Planet's overview of Italy to learn even more about the country's history: http://www.lonelyplanet.com/italy/history.

Books

Beer, Eugen. *Italy: History and Landscape*. New York: Barnes & Noble, 2010.

Di Palo, Lou. *Di Palo's Guide to the Essential Foods of Italy: 100 Years of Wisdom and Stories from Behind the Counter*. New York: Ballantine Books, 2014.

Fili, Louise. *Italianissimo: The Quintessential Guide to What Italians Do Best*. New York: Little Bookroom, 2008.

Parasecoli, Fabio. *Al Dente: A History of Food in Italy*. London: Reaktion Books, 2014.

Whittaker, Andrew. *Speak the Culture: Italy*. London: Thorogood, 2010.

NOTE TO EDUCATORS: This book contains both imperial and metric measurements as well as references to global practices and trends in an effort to encourage the student to gain a worldly perspective. We, as publishers, feel it's our role to give young adults the tools they need to thrive in a global society.

SERIES GLOSSARY

ancestral: relating to ancestors, or relatives who have lived in the past.

archaeologist: a scientist that investigates past societies by digging in the earth to examine their remains.

artisanal: describing something produced on a small scale, usually handmade by skilled craftspeople.

colony: a settlement in another country or place that is controlled by a "home" country.

commonwealth: an association of sovereign nations unified by common cultural, political, and economic interests and traits.

communism: a social and economic philosophy characterized by a classless society and the absence of private property.

continent: any of the seven large land masses that constitute most of the dry land on the surface of the earth.

cosmopolitan: worldly; showing the influence of many cultures.

culinary: relating to the kitchen, cookery, and style of eating.

cultivated: planted and harvested for food, as opposed to the growth of plants in the wild.

currency: a system of money.

demographics: the study of population trends.

denomination: a religious grouping within a faith that has its own organization.

dynasty: a ruling family that extends across generations, usually in an autocratic form of government, such as a monarchy.

ecosystems: environments where interdependent organisms live.

endemic: native, or not introduced, to a particular region, and not naturally found in other areas.

exile: absence from one's country or home, usually enforced by a government for political or religious reasons.

feudal: a system of economic, political, or social organization in which poor landholders are subservient to wealthy landlords; used mostly in relation to the Middle Ages.

globalization: the processes relating to increasing international exchange that have resulted in faster, easier connections across the world.

gross national product: the measure of all the products and services a country produces in a year.

heritage: tradition and history.

homogenization: the process of blending elements together, sometimes resulting in a less interesting mixture.

iconic: relating to something that has become an emblem or symbol.

idiom: the language particular to a community or class; usually refers to regular, "everyday" speech.

immigrants: people who move to and settle in a new country.

indigenous: originating in and naturally from a particular region or country.

industrialization: the process by which a country changes from a farming society to one that is based on industry and manufacturing.

SERIES GLOSSARY

integration: the process of opening up a place, community, or organization to all types of people.

kinship: web of social relationships that have a common origin derived from ancestors and family.

literacy rate: the percentage of people who can read and write.

matriarchal: of or relating to female leadership within a particular group or system.

migrant: a person who moves from one place to another, usually for reasons of employment or economic improvement.

militarized: warlike or military in character and thought.

missionary: one who goes on a journey to spread a religion.

monopoly: a situation where one company or state controls the market for an industry or product.

natural resources: naturally occurring materials, such as oil, coal, and gold, that can be used by people.

nomadic: describing a way of life in which people move, usually seasonally, from place to place in search of food, water, and pastureland.

nomadic: relating to people who have no fixed residence and move from place to place.

parliament: a body of government responsible for enacting laws.

patriarchal: of or relating to male leadership within a particular group or system.

patrilineal: relating to the relationship based on the father or the descendants through the male line.

polygamy: the practice of having more than one spouse.

provincial: belonging to a province or region outside of the main cities of a country.

racism: prejudice or animosity against people belonging to other races.

ritualize: to mark or perform with specific behaviors or observances.

sector: part or aspect of something, especially of a country's or region's economy.

secular: relating to worldly concerns; not religious.

societal: relating to the order, structure, or functioning of society or community.

socioeconomic: relating to social and economic factors, such as education and income, often used when discussing how classes, or levels of society, are formed.

statecraft: the ideas about and methods of running a government.

traditional: relating to something that is based on old historical ways of doing things.

urban sprawl: the uncontrolled expansion of urban areas away from the center of the city into remote, outlying areas.

urbanization: the increasing movement of people from rural areas to cities, usually in search of economic improvement, and the conditions resulting this migration.

INDEX

INDEX

INDEX

INDEX

PHOTO CREDITS

Page	Page Location	Archive/Photographer	Page	Page Location	Archive/Photographer
6	Full page	Dreamstime/Tomas Marek	31	Bottom	Dollar Photo Club/Jacek Chabraszewski
8	Top	Dollar Photo Club/Tupungato	32	Top	Wikimedia Commons/Gaspa
10	Top left	Dollar Photo Club/Robbic	34	Middle	iStock.com/starmaro
11	Top	Dollar Photo Club/PicturePast	35	Bottom	iStock.com/YinYang
12	Top	Dollar Photo Club/kent196	36	Bottom	Dollar Photo Club/Robert Crum
13	Middle	Dollar Photo Club/creedline	38	Bottom	Dollar Photo Club/Pavel Losevsky
14	Bottom	Dollar Photo Club/Rick Henzel	39	Bottom	Dollar Photo Club/Joshua Rainey
15	Bottom	Dollar Photo Club/Perseomedusa	40	Top	Dreamstime/Mario Bonotto
16	Top	iStock.com/guenterguni	42	Top left	Wikimedia Commons/Bain Photo Service
18	Top	Dollar Photo Club/frenk58	42	Top right	iStock.com/ermess
19	Bottom	iStock.com/TerryJ	43	Bottom	Dollar Photo Club/lapas77
20	Top	Dreamstime/Annworthy	45	Top right	Dollar Photo Club/scerpica
21	Bottom left	Dollar Photo Club/Jaimie Duplass	46	Top	Dollar Photo Club/Amro
21	Bottom middle	Dollar Photo Club/fusolino	47	Bottom	Dollar Photo Club/lapas77
21	Bottom right	Dollar Photo Club/generalfmv	48	Top	Dollar Photo Club/lenagi
22	Top	Flickr	50	Top left	Dollar Photo Club/Jenifoto
23	Bottom	Dollar Photo Club/vision images	50	Top right	Dollar Photo Club/Gabriele Maltinti
24	Top	Dollar Photo Club/dusk	51	Bottom	Dollar Photo Club/fusolino
26	Top	Dreamstime/Konstantinos Papaioannou	53	Top	Dollar Photo Club/Freesurf
26	Bottom	Dollar Photo Club/Hoda Bogdan	53	Bottom left	Dollar Photo Club/KaferPhoto
27	Top left	Dollar Photo Club/Comugnero Silvana	54	Top	Dollar Photo Club/MasterLu
27	Top right	Dollar Photo Club/al62	55	Bottom	Dollar Photo Club/Tetiana Zbrodko
28	Top left	Dreamstime/Photographerlondon			
29	Bottom	Dollar Photo Club/photopitu			
30	Top	Dollar Photo Club/Pixelshop			

COVER

Top	freeimages/eschu1952
Bottom left	freeimages/nkzs
Bottom right	Dreamstime/Mario Bonotto

ABOUT THE AUTHOR

Michael Centore is a writer and editor. He has helped produce many titles, including memoirs, cookbooks, and educational materials, among others, for a variety of publishers. He has experience in several facets of book production, from photo research to fact checking. His poetry and essays have appeared in *Crux*, *Tight*, *Mockingbird*, and other print- and web-based publications. Prior to his involvement in publishing, he worked as a stone mason, art handler, and housepainter. He was born in Hartford, Connecticut, and lives in Brooklyn, New York.